THE KLONDIKE GOLD RUSH

A BOOK OF POSTCARDS

*"The inhumanity which this trail has been
witness to, the heartbreak and suffering which
so many have undergone, cannot be imagined."*
Clifford Sifton,
Canadian Minister of the Interior, 1898

D1089018

**Canadian Cataloguing in
Publication Data**
Wilson, Graham, 1962-
The Klondike Gold Rush :
A Book of Postcards

ISBN 0-9681955-1-2
1. Klondike River Valley
(Yukon)--Gold discoveries--
Pictorial works. 2.
Klondike River Valley
(Yukon)--Gold discoveries.
3. Postcards--Yukon--
Klondike River Valley.
I. Title.

FC4022.3.W537 1997
971.9'1   C97-900568-X
F1095.K5W53 1997

To order prints of any of the
photographs in this
collection contact Wolf
Creek Books. Please allow 6
to 8 weeks for shipping. To
place an order call (403)668-
4260 or write to Box 31275,
211 Main Street, Whitehorse,
Yukon, Y1A 5P7 or e-mail us
at Wcreek@hypertech.yk.ca.

**WOLF CREEK
BOOKS**

When the small steamship *Excelsior* docked in San Francisco in July 1897, the world was watching. Aboard this vessel were millionaires who had been penniless men only months before. As these scruffy miners swaggered down the gangplank carrying jars, satchels and cases filled with gold, more than five thousand people crowded the docks and cheered.

A few days later the steamship *Portland* landed at Seattle with sixty-eight miners and almost a ton of gold. The news of the find grabbed newspaper headlines and was on everyone's lips. Overnight, the word *Klondike* took on mythic proportions.

Within days thousands flocked to west coast towns from San Francisco to Vancouver trying to book passage north. The fact that the Klondike was more than fifteen hundred miles away and over a precipitous mountain pass would not deter many. Gold fever had grasped the nation, and everyone wanted the chance to try their luck in the new frontier.

The stampeders faced one of the most arduous treks imaginable. They traveled up the coast in overcrowded and often decrepit ships. They spent the winter ferrying supplies over the cold and dangerous Chilkoot Pass and built rickety boats and navigated the lakes and rapids of the Yukon River.

Most stampeders arrived in

Dawson in the spring and summer of 1898. They wandered into this carnival-like town exhausted from their journey. There are many stories of stampeders who upon arriving in Dawson immediately booked passage home, so travel weary and worn-out they did not have any energy to even try to work a claim.

Most of the population of Dawson dined on beans and pancakes. They slept in canvas tents and spent their days in idle anticipation of finding their fortune. They had endured the most difficult experience of their life just getting to the Klondike valley. Now they were idle with little opportunity to stake or even work someone's claim.

The irony of the Klondike Gold Rush was that the gold fields had been almost entirely staked the year before the stampeders arrived. There was little opportunity for day laborers and many stampeders were flat broke. Dawson was a boom town where the fabulously rich and the dirt poor walked the same wooden planks over the marshy streets. Despair was everywhere except in the dance halls, saloons and shops.

The vast majority of the stampeders left the Yukon without making a cent. Returning home would present many challenges, but these would pale in comparison to what they had endured. They had experienced the adventure of a lifetime.

The Klondike Gold Rush

Steamship "City of Seattle" in Glacier Bay, Alaska, with Muir Glacier in the background,. Steamships such as this carried thousands of stampeders to Alaska, c.1898.
Yukon Archives, H.C. Barley Collection

Wolf Creek Books Inc., Whitehorse, Yukon

The Klondike Gold Rush

Stampeders amid mountains of supplies landed at the mouth of the Taiya River near Dyea, Alaska. Each stampeder carried almost a ton of supplies over the Chilkoot Trail, c.1898.

Yukon Archives, Winter & Pond Collection

Wolf Creek Books Inc., Whitehorse, Yukon

The Klondike Gold Rush

A dog team in front of Case & Draper Photography store in Skagway, Alaska, c. 1898.
MacBride Museum Collection

Wolf Creek Books Inc., Whitehorse, Yukon

The Klondike Gold Rush

The muddy mainstreet of Dyea, Alaska. Little remains of Dyea today, c.1898.
University of Washington, E.A. Hegg Collection

Wolf Creek Books Inc., Whitehorse, Yukon

The Klondike Gold Rush

*Family carrying heavy packs and pulling a handcart
at the start of the Chilkoot Trail, c.1897.
MacBride Museum Collection.*

Wolf Creek Books Inc., Whitehorse, Yukon

The Klondike Gold Rush

"Chilkoot Jack," a Chilkat Indian Chief, guided many over the Chilkoot Pass to the Yukon. He is pictured here wearing ceremonial dress, c. 1898. Yukon Archives, Vogee Collection

Wolf Creek Books Inc., Whitehorse, Yukon

The Klondike Gold Rush

Stampeders hauling sleds up "Jacob's Ladder," in a canyon on the Chilkoot Trail, near Skagway, Alaska, c.1898.
Yukon Archives, Winter and Pond Collection.

Wolf Creek Books Inc., Whitehorse, Yukon

The Klondike Gold Rush

Stampeders climbing the "Golden Stairs" to the Chilkoot summit, Alaska, c.1898. MacBride Museum Collection

Wolf Creek Books Inc., Whitehorse, Yukon

On Chilkoot Pass

The Klondike Gold Rush

Stampeders ascending the Chilkoot summit single file.
This climb was known as the "Golden Stair," c.1898.
University of Washington

Wolf Creek Books Inc., Whitehorse, Yukon

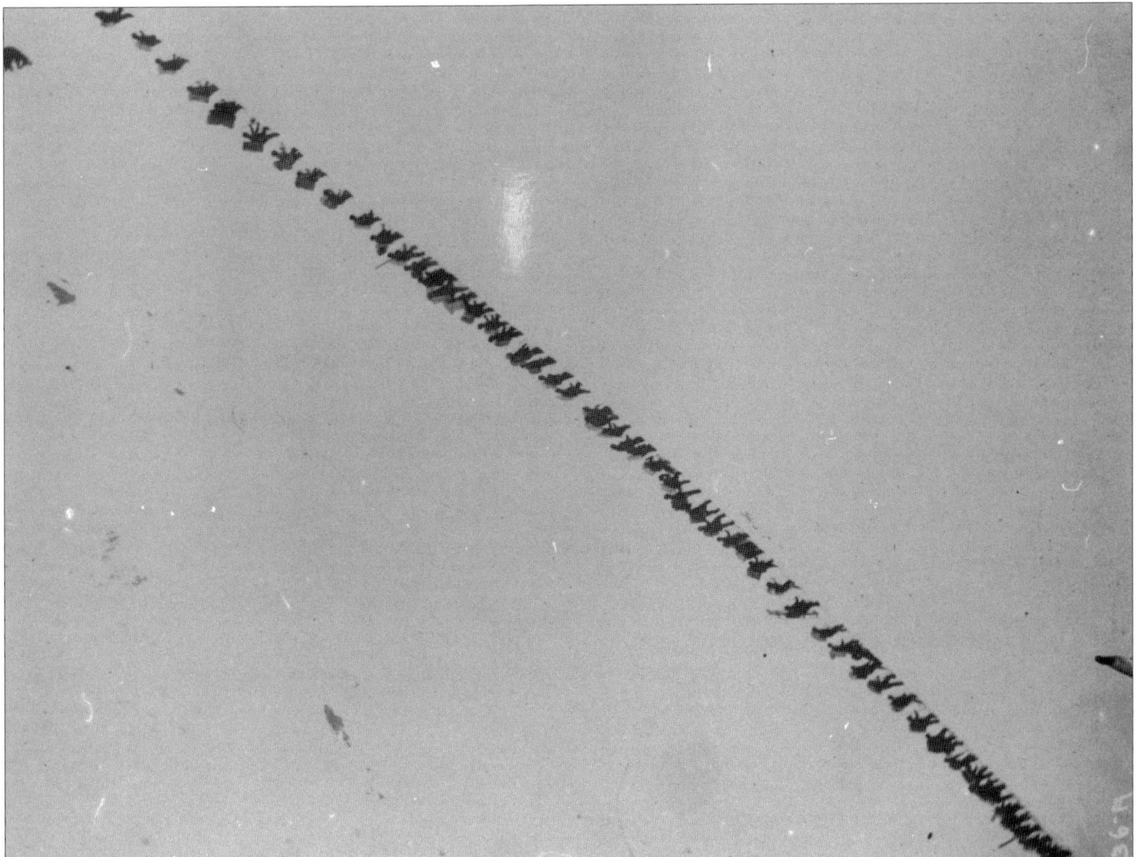

The Klondike Gold Rush

Stampeders form a thin black line as they struggle up to the summit of the Chilkoot Pass, Alaska, c. 1898. University of Washington, E.A. Hegg Collection

Wolf Creek Books Inc., Whitehorse, Yukon

BOUNDARY LINE ON CHILKOOT PASS ALASKA

The Klondike Gold Rush

Tent camp at the summit of the Chilkoot Pass. This icy camp was frequently buried by blizzards and became a makeshift border between Canada and the US, c.1898.

University of Washington, E.A. Hegg Collection

Wolf Creek Books Inc., Whitehorse, Yukon

The Klondike Gold Rush

A group of stampeders with loaded sleds and caches of supplies on the Chilkoot summit, Alaska/Canada border, c.1897.

Alaska Historical Library Collection

Wolf Creek Books Inc., Whitehorse, Yukon

The Klondike Gold Rush

Boat-building among the mass of tents on the shores of Lake Bennett during the spring of 1898. More than 20,000 people with little or no experience built 7,000 boats at the headwaters of the Yukon River. Vancouver Public Library Collection

Wolf Creek Books Inc., Whitehorse, Yukon

The Klondike Gold Rush

Stampeders pulling a boat by rope from shore while the men in the boat help with poles on Tagish Lake, Yukon. Other boats are visible in background, c. 1898.
Vancouver Public Library

Wolf Creek Books Inc., Whitehorse, Yukon

The Klondike Gold Rush

*Stampeders running treacherous Miles Canyon on the
Yukon River near Whitehorse, Yukon, c. 1898.
Yukon Archives, Vogee Collection*

Wolf Creek Books Inc., Whitehorse, Yukon

The Klondike Gold Rush

Underground miners working by candlelight in
claustrophobic tunnels near Dawson City, Yukon,
c. 1898.

University of Washington, E.A. Hegg Collection

Wolf Creek Books Inc., Whitehorse, Yukon

The Klondike Gold Rush

Meals tended to be simple and repetitous for most stampeders and often comprised of beans, pancakes or dried meat, c. 1898.
Yukon Archives

Wolf Creek Books Inc., Whitehorse, Yukon

The Klondike Gold Rush

Panning for gold on Bonanza Creek, Yukon.
Yukon Archives, McLennan Collection, c. 1898.

Wolf Creek Books Inc., Whitehorse, Yukon

THE PROSPECTOR

The Klondike Gold Rush

Prospecting for gold was often solitary, back-breaking work, c. 1898.

Vancouver Public Library

Wolf Creek Books Inc., Whitehorse, Yukon

The Klondike Gold Rush

Rockerboxes were commonly used to retrieve gold from the dirt and gravel of Bonanza Creek, Yukon, c. 1898.

Yukon Archives, H.C. Barley Collection

Wolf Creek Books Inc., Whitehorse, Yukon

The Klondike Gold Rush

Mrs. G.I. Lowe's laundry on Bonanza Creek, near Dawson City. She also did free mending and told fortunes and was a very successful entrepreneur, c.1898.

University of Washington, E.A. Hegg Collection

Wolf Creek Books Inc., Whitehorse, Yukon

The Klondike Gold Rush

Interior of a store with a man pouring gold dust from a pouch to be weighed on a set of gold scales. Gold dust was an accepted currency in Dawson City, Yukon, c.1898.

MacBride Museum Collection

Wolf Creek Books Inc., Whitehorse, Yukon

The Klondike Gold Rush

July 4th celebrations of Independence Day were observed in Dawson City. Most stampeders were US citizens, c.1898.

Yukon Archives, McLennan Collection

Wolf Creek Books Inc., Whitehorse, Yukon

The Klondike Gold Rush

A tent store specializing in fresh lemonade. Stores such as this could earn their proprietors a small fortune and were popular in Dawson City, Yukon, c. 1898.

Vancouver Public Library Collection

Wolf Creek Books Inc., Whitehorse, Yukon

The Klondike Gold Rush

Prostitutes holding puppies, gathered for a "drinking bee" in the White Chapel district of Dawson City, Yukon, c.1898.
MacBride Museum Collection

Wolf Creek Books Inc., Whitehorse, Yukon

The Klondike Gold Rush

Receiving mail in Dawson City was an event for a town filled with homesick stampeders, c. 1898.
University of Washington, E.A. Hegg Collection

Wolf Creek Books Inc., Whitehorse, Yukon